A Spiritual Journey Out of Depression

(Through prose and poetry)

Travelled By S. L. Kuno

◆ FriesenPress

One Printers Way
Altona, MB R0G 0B0
Canada

www.friesenpress.com

ISBN
978-1-03-916904-3 (Hardcover)
978-1-03-916903-6 (Paperback)
978-1-03-916905-0 (eBook)

1. RELIGION, CHRISTIAN LIFE, INSPIRATIONAL

Distributed to the trade by The Ingram Book Company

Table of Contents

Dedication   vi

Thank you   vii

Introduction   ix
    The Background to this Journey   x
    The Garden and the Gardener   xii

Depression   1
    The Hole in my Soul   2
    Suit of Armour   5
    The Closet   6
    Exhaustion   7
    Dust   8
    Stuffed in a Box   9
    Colours   11
    Do I Know my own Heart?   13
    Demons of Depression   14
    What Others See   15

Healing   17
    The Simplest Prayer   18
    My Dependants   19
    Living Water   20
    Loaf of Bread   21
    The Wound   22

Rebellion   23
    Bumblebee   24

Disobedience   25
Busy   26
I'm a Little Potsherd   28

Trust & Surrender   **29**
Trust   30
The Filter   32
The Coat   34
The Anchor   35
Surrender   36
Obedience   37
The Cliff   39

Redemption   **41**
The Gift   42
Half-Buried   45
Stone Fountain   46
My Walk   47
Circle   49
Christ in Me   50

Faithfulness   **51**
Leave and Forsake   52
Where are You?   53
My Prayer   54
Mirror   55
I Know You are There   56
The Mustard Seed   58

Forgiveness   **61**
Dagger to the Heart   62
What Might Have Been   64
Ball of String   66
What is Seen   67

Transformation   **69**
    Burrs   70
    Growing Pains   72
    Two Ways   73
    Caterpillar, Chrysalis, Butterfly   76
    Fill Me   78
    Die to Self   80
    Purpose   82
    Broken Vessels   84
    Your Love Rains Down   85
    The Flame   86
    An I for an Aye   87

Who God Is   **89**
    Created in Your Image   90
    Fire   92
    Who am I   93
    Words   94
    Eternal Life   96
    You Are The One   97
    Love Says   98

Thankfulness   **99**
    Morning Song   100
    Because   102
    Thank you   103
    "My Beautiful Child"   104
    Wealth   105
    The Shore   107

A Final Message   **109**
    Sea of Trouble   110

Dedication

These writings all belong to the Lord.

These are the words that flow through me. These are my conversations, questions, and observations with the Lord. Filtered through my limited understanding. They are neither perfect nor complete but they are undeniably heartfelt. Some are more spirit-driven and some are just cries from my heart.

All belong to the Lord,

For the Lord's purpose,

For the Lord's glory.

Thank you

To all those who have walked this journey with me, whether they knew it or not.

To family and friends, to peers and bible study groups,

To co-workers and counsellors, both formal and informal.

You have all walked this journey with me, whether *I* knew it or not.

To all who have encouraged the sharing of this journey, my story thus far.

For prayers, and laughter, and tears,

For advice, and the practicalities of book publishing.

I could not have done it without you.

The biggest thank you goes to God

For the love bestowed upon me,

Thank you is too small of a word.

Introduction

The Background
to this Journey

I have lived with depression from my mid-teens until my mid-fifties, four decades. (By the way, that is the same length of time the Israelites wandered the desert)

I have been suicidal three times, with idealization and plans but just stopping short of implementation. The first when I was in high school, the second time in my mid-thirtys, and the third time in my early fiftys.

Just so you know, it is a myth that you need a reason to be depressed. I had no reason. I came from a loving two-parent family, was not abused, was financially stable, had many friends and was not bullied. I have a loving husband, two well-adjusted sons, a beautiful home, and a respected career as a registered nurse. See, nothing to be depressed about, except depression doesn't care about any of that. Chronic depression is not about your circumstances. It is a disorder involving the way you think and the way you perceive the world.

Now don't get me wrong, I had many happy times and genuine love and laughter in my life. It wasn't all depression, but when depression was there it took over completely.

It was not until I was fifty-five and had arranged a mental health counsellor as a guest speaker for a group of clients that I recognized it in myself. Basically he talked about depression not as anyone's fault but as a health disorder similar to any other health condition. For me that was the light-bulb moment. It took away the stigma of seeking help and treatment. It also relieved the burden and energy of hiding and pretending everything was *sunshine and lollipops.*

I started medication, found a Christian counsellor (actually, God provided that connection for me), took a medical leave of absence from work and finally took ownership of the fact that I have a medical condition called depression. No more denial.

At this time I have never felt better in my life! And this is admidst a pandemic, lockdowns, and uncertainty. I am at peace, and experience a sense of joy for each new day. (Just like entering the promised land of milk and honey.)

I'm not sure if this is a cure or remission. But even if it is remission, I know feeling that sense of depression is not normal and I am no longer ashamed to ask for help, be it counselling or medication or a combination.

Thank you Lord! I couldn't have done it without you.

What follows is my spiritual journey out of depression.

The Garden and the Gardener

For the past three days, I have been frantically gardening, weeding, pruning, cutting, and mulching.

And today, I thought this is mirroring what has been happening within me as well. Through counselling, reading, praying, and writing, I have been gardening my soul. Pulling out the thoughts and feelings that have been keeping me trapped and have been choking the life out of me. Stuck in a place where I literally could not see the forest for the trees. By pruning away the negative emotions and disentangling from the negative talk, I am allowing the light and air to flow through.

By forgiving and asking for forgiveness the dead-fall that has been weighing me down, suffocating me, has been lifted.

By asking for prayer, surrounding myself with supportive, understanding people who have faith, and reading the bible and Christian books on the subject, I feel cared for. (A lot like mulch.)

By doing all this I can see the beginnings of the beauty that is my soul. And what a beautiful garden it will be!

August 2019

The Journey begins...

Depression

"I loathe my very life;
Therefore I will give free rein to my complaint
And I will speak out in the bitterness of my soul."

Job 10 : 1(NIV)

The Hole in my Soul

There is a hole in my soul.

A dark gaping wound.

A deep, yearning ache.

It hurts.

The pain overwhelms,

It sucks the colour out of life:

Everything turns to shades of dullest grey,

It bleeds the musical notes from the air.

All I hear is an ongoing monotonous hum.

The stench of rotting decay fills my nostrils –

It is so strong I taste the bitterness of it.

A layer of ash covers everything I touch.

I can't feel anything.

There is a deep yearning, a wanting I can't explain. I look to fill this hole, but nothing soothes, nothing relieves the burn in my soul.

Not alcohol, food nor drugs.

Not work, hobbies, nor entertainment.

Not sex, nor material goods.

Not family nor friends.

Nothing fills the void. Nothing satisfies.

The longer the hole is there the larger it grows.

It is consuming me.

Soon the hole will swallow me.

The dullness of my eyes cannot see any glimmer of light. My ears no longer hear anything but the hum. I am completely broken.

Please, can you mend this hole? Can you fix the brokenness that is me? Is there a remedy, an ointment, a balm for this heart-wrenching ache that fills my soul? Please, I beg of you.

Your loving hands lift me up. Gently, You wash the layers of this world from my ears, my eyes, my mouth and nose. Gradually, I begin to sense that what my soul is missing can only come from You.

I hunger and thirst for more.

Please fill my cup. Mend my soul. I wish to be complete, whole. I wish to be led through green pastures and beside still waters. I wish to know the peace that passes all understanding.

You provide the colour and music to my soul. As I draw closer the hurt and pain fades. Falling off me like drops of tar. Slowly at first, but picking up speed as your radiant glow penetrates my innermost being. Filling every nook and cranny of what is me.

It even overfills me. It leaks out for others to see, and hear, and wonder, what the mysterious sparkle is.

Thank you is insufficient to express the gratitude I feel. Your love and kindness leaves me in awe.

In awesome wonder, How Great Thou Art.

Suit of Armour

I wear a suit of armour.

It is bright, it is shiny, it is strong.

It protects, it deflects, it is safe.

It is heavy, it is cumbersome, it is stifling.

It is all I've ever known.

Without it I am open, exposed, vulnerable.

And that is terrifying.

The Closet

For over forty years, I have hidden. I hid in a small, cramped closet. Not revealing myself to anyone, hiding even from myself.

Afraid I will not be accepted, will not be loved or wanted, not even sure if I could love or accept myself.

I had heard, I had read, and intellectually *knew,* but did not accept the fact that God loves me absolutely and unconditionally.

Why would I reject that? Why could I not believe that? Why did I fear that? Why would I not accept unconditional love?

I've acted like a small child covering my eyes. If I can't see You, then I remain unseen. And I believed I could hide. That the God that formed me, knew me before creation itself, would not know the parts of me that I had tucked away, covered up, buried, and sealed within myself.

What a heavy burden – crippling, soul crushing, wearisome and lonely.

I WANT OUT OF THIS SMALL, CRAMPED CLOSET!!

Lord, I give it all to You. I believe … help my unbelief.

Exhaustion

Bone crushing exhaustion

Each muscle like jelly

An inner will lying in tatters

The only sensation left is one of dried saltiness
along old tear tracks

Failure permeates the air

Dust

Particles of dust swirl and twirl and spin

Around and around they fly

Creating their own momentum

Feeding off their own energy

First we are observers, and then we are drawn into the dance, participating with the grains of twirling and spinning granules, providing them strength and power, faster and faster they move, until we are no longer in control, we are no longer a dance partner, but an unwilling participant.

The savageness of them hits us, producing sharp and stinging bites, over and over it is repeated, until the only sensation is pain and misery.

We lie beaten and battered and broken

Sandblasted by our own creation

Sandblasted by our own thoughts

"...but be transformed by the renewing of your mind." Romans 12:2 (NIV)

Stuffed in a Box

I have *stuffed* my emotions, feelings, opinions, ideas, goals and dreams in a *box* for forty plus years, until the box burst. All these things are now scattered about the room. The floor is covered and *stuff* is littered about – the box is empty but the room is a mess. It is everywhere. I look at it and don't know what to do with it, where to begin. I want to shove it all back in the box, but it won't fit and the lid is broken.

When I show this room to others I feel vulnerable. Comments of: "What a mess!", "What are you going to do with that?", "Why would you keep it?", "That should be thrown out!", and "This just needs to be cleaned up!", throw me into a panic. Why would I share this with anyone? I feel overwhelmed. My chest hurts. I don't want to deal with this, any of it – THROW IT BACK IN THE BOX!

I pick up an item but am reluctant to part with it. What if I need it? What would I be without it? I am filled with inertia, fear, shame and doubt. I don't know what to do. I sit in the middle of this mess and cry. PLEASE let's lock the door to this room.

Who would understand this? Who would help me?

God walks into my room and sees me.

As I focus on the *stuff*, the mess scattered about, and the broken empty box, frantically waving my arms about, trying to explain, reason and rationalize the situation, God sees me.

As I ask why can't I just get a bigger box, and why would anyone want an empty box, especially if it is broken, God sees me.

Those patient, understanding, kind, and loving eyes do not see the mess, the *stuff* that is scattered all over the floor, the heaps, the piles, the tattered, the broken, the discarded things of my life lying all over the place. Those eyes never leave my face – that smile sees only me. I am the Holy One's child and I am loved totally and unconditionally not for my *stuff* and *things*, but for my being a child of God.

Colours

An inky indigo

Deep in darkness

Unable to judge its depth

An unending sea of blue

If one stares long enough, other shades seep through, but always blue

It is easy to be drawn in

To lose one's self

To drown in this sea of blue, formed by tears

But I resist, longing for another colour, a change. There must be more...

A fire engine red appears

A hot, burning that surfaces from the blue

A blazing spark shooting rich red

Full of energy and anger

Melting the blue away, consuming it

The red reflects off of every surface

But still I long for another colour. There must be more...

I watch the destruction of the red, a flash as it burns itself out

A brilliant yellow rises from the centre of it all

So beautiful and bright it is difficult to gaze directly upon it

The shafts of golden yellow are flowing everywhere

Creating a glittering mass of colour as it goes

Calming the red and energizing the blue

A kaleidoscope of every colour: purple, orange, and green as well as blue, red and yellow

All shades, all tones and all hues fill the senses

The strength and beauty overwhelms, uplifts, overflows and satisfies a longing desire

It is complete

The colour yellow required the blue and red I held to create the complete picture

I only needed to surrender it

Do I Know my own Heart?

I hover over the heart-shaped pool – smooth liquid surface reflecting like a silver mirror. The beauty of it takes the breath away. Do I know this heart? What lies beneath the surface? It is an enigma. All questions – no discernible answers.

With timid fingers, I gently touch the surface leaving a trail and gentle ripples that slip into the solid-looking surface once again.

No way to judge the depth. No way to see anything other than the reflective surface.

What does it hold? What is under the seen? What is beyond the known?

The curiosity mounts, the questions stack one upon another. I want to know what the heart holds. I want to know its depth, what is under the surface.

But I am unable, not wanting to break the surface, to dive beneath the known, to go beyond the present.

I am afraid I will be overtaken by the depths of my own heart. I am afraid if it is let free it will wash over and wash away those closest to me in a flood of emotion.

Best to keep it restrained, controlled and unexplored?

Demons of Depression

The demons of depression have been attacking again. They are named self-pity, doubt, despair, guilt, hopelessness, failure, self-preservation, withdrawal, isolation and loneliness.

They swarm my mind, my body, my heart. With piercing needles they drive hot burning thoughts and ideas, both shallow and deep they penetrate. Attacking my most vulnerable points – areas they have attacked before – my points of weakness. They relentlessly and viciously attack. They are overwhelming and weigh heavily upon me. Wanting me to lie down and give up, but I do not wish to return to that place. I do not wish to travel that well-worn road that I have traversed many times before. I choose not to go. And I possess the tools, the understanding and the discernment, the Lord has provided me. I possess the courage, the strength and the overflowing love of the Holy Spirit that resides within me. I draw on all those resources. I draw on the name and blood of Jesus.

And I take a round mouth shovel and wack them back. I smash them on the tops of their heads. I twirl with my shovel at arm's length and they are beaten back and knocked down. Again and again I wallop them, forcing them from me. They leave defeated for now.

They did have me surrounded, their bodies creating a barrier of darkness – empty blackness that sucks the life from me. Now that they are gone the light floods in.

By embracing the flame of Christ within me, I am able to clear the way to the greater light beyond me.

What Others See

What do others see when they look at me?
I do not recognize the person they describe.
That person has so many wonderful attributes.
So positive.
Why do I not know that person?
Why can't I see that person?

The person I see and know is insecure, full of doubt, hateful, lashing out at anything or anyone that gets too close, is negative, withdraws and pushes away.

I would like to meet the person that others describe as me. Why have I neither accepted, nor embraced that person? Why do I reject myself, push myself away?

How do I move forward from here?

The answer of course is acceptance of who I am.

A complex being – with both the positive and the negative. Neither all one nor all the other. Rejecting either the positive or negative aspects of myself creates only pain. Like ripping myself in half. Neither can survive without the other. I have spent years rejecting the positive in myself and have lived a painful, lonely and dark life thus far. It does not work. Time to try something new.

Rejecting the negative to embrace the positive would create an equally failing existence, because I would have to hide and deny that the negative exists. That is not a viable option.

Learning to knit both halves together into one cohesive being. I would like to try that.

Learning to acknowledge myself, learning to accept myself, learning to love myself.

Healing

He lifted me out of the slimy pit,
Out of the mud and mire;
He set my feet on a rock
and gave me a firm place to stand.

Psalm 40:2 (NIV)

The Simplest Prayer

"HELP"

(Oh, **H**oly One,

Everlasting **L**ove

Please)

I encourage you to try it

Loaf of Bread

Think of a loaf of bread, fresh from the oven. A warm, delicious yeast smell. A toasted golden top. When gently rapped upon, a hollow sound is produced. It is whole – one piece.

This loaf does not provide nourishment until it is broken and internalized. Just like Jesus.

"I am the bread of life." John 6:35 (NIV)

The Wound

The wound ran deep. The object that caused the wound remained embedded. It was sharp and jagged and fragmented. Over time it became encapsulated, surrounded by layers of scar tissue and inflammation as the body tried to protect itself.

Certain movements, positions and postures caused it to flare and another layer of scar tissue was added. Becoming larger each and every time – gradually reaching the point where it no longer was the object causing the pain and suffering but the protective coating itself. No longer the original sin but the self lies, denials and cover-ups.

Family and friends intercede with prayers and love for removal and healing. The Lord is able to reach down and remove the foreign body, to remove the inflammation and the layers and layers of scar tissue. Its removal will leave a large open hole.

That empty space is now able to receive the precious Holy Spirit. That hole to be filled with love, light, joy, and the over-abundance of forgiveness.

Are you ready?

Just open your hands and release it to the Lord.

Just open your heart and offer it all to the Lord.

Just open your lips and pour forth your confession.

Then you will receive the healing. Then you will receive the good gifts the Lord offers.

It will be more than you could ask for or imagine.

Rebellion

The mind governed by the flesh is hostile to God;
it does not submit to God's law, nor can it do so.
Those who are in the realm of the flesh cannot
please God.

Romans 8: 7&8 (NIV)

Bumblebee

Watched a bumblebee bang himself against the window. Over and over he tried – probably seeing a reflection in the window. But he was rebuffed time and time again.

I laugh and I think how foolish!

And then I think ...

I do that. I have done that many times in my life. Bang myself against a reflection, trying to find passage through, only to be rebuffed and not understanding why. Again and again.

How foolish!

Disobedience

Wilful defiance

Disobedience

Nope, Can't do, Won't do, Busy

Won't work, Impossible

Disobedience

Not me, Can't hear you, Go away

Disobedience

Run, Hide, Get someone else

Disobedience

Can't you see I'm busy doing?

And I'm doing it all for you?

I don't have time to do that!

It doesn't fit into my plans.

That is not something I would ever do anyways.

I have no ability to do it!

I don't know how to do it!

Why are you asking me?

Disobedience

Busy

Busy, hurry, scurry
Go, go, go ...
Do, do, do ...

Appointments, dates, schedules
Go faster, do more, work harder

"Help me, Lord!" I call
"listen"

Busy, hurry, scurry
Go, go, go ...
Do, do, do ...

Meetings, committees, reports
Go faster, do more, work harder

"Help me, Lord!" I call
"listen"

Busy, hurry, scurry
Go, go, go ...
Do, do, do ...

Deadlines, commitments, responsibilities
Go faster, do more, work harder

"Help me, Lord!" I call
"Listen"

Busy, hurry, scurry
Go, go, go ...
Do, do, do ...

Work, home, community
Go faster, do more, work harder

"Help me, Lord!" I call
"listen"

Busy, hurry, scurry
Go, go, go ...
Do, do, do ...

Family, church, relationships
Go faster, do more, work harder

"Help me, Lord!" I call
"listen"

...Busy ... Go... Do...
"and rest in Me."

"Come with me by yourselves to a quiet place and get some rest." Mark 6:31 (NIV)

I'm a Little Potsherd

(To be sung to the tune of I'm a little tea pot)

I'm a little potsherd

Scattered all about

Hear me question

Hear me doubt

That is when I'm picked up

In the potter's hand

To know my Master and to understand

**"Woe to him who quarrels with his Maker,
To him who is but a potsherd among the potsherds on the
ground." Isaiah 45:9 (NIV)**

Trust & Surrender

Trust in the Lord with all your heart and lean not
on your own understanding;
In all your ways acknowledge him, and he will
make your paths straight.

Proverbs 3 : 5&6 (NIV)

Trust

What a full and meaningful word

Trust

5 letters – R, S, T, T, U

In order, near the end of the alphabet,

Trust

Begins and ends with T

Lower case t, like a small cross

With U in the middle

Trust

One syllable

With YOU in the middle

A single vowel surrounded by consonants

Like a circle, with YOU as a single point on which to focus

Trust

It is deep with meaning

Trust

For such a small word, how can it be so encompassing?

So filled with promise?

Trust

How can one word twist me in such knots?

How can it pull me in so many directions at once?

And yet fill me with inertia?

Trust

For such a simple word, how can it be so complex?

The Filter

Broken strands of understanding float through the air.

We each wear a filter manufactured from our upbringing, our life experiences, and what we feed on. Through this filter we experience our surroundings, the relationships to all others including You, and how we envision the world.

The filter can be nothing but faulty, as it has been made by us. We each scramble for the truth, but only look for the version that fits our filter.

We fight, accuse, dismiss, sit in our self-righteousness, and judge. Believing we hold the key to understanding and truth, but we don't.

To truly understand and know the truth we must first remove the filter. Even before that, though, we must first realize we wear a filter.

Dear Lord:

Please remove the filter I have made. Please be gentle as I am scared. It is how I have lived my life. When it is removed those broken strands of understanding may fit in ways that I could never have imagined. I would have to accept that my thoughts, ideas and concepts of You, of Jesus, of the Holy Spirit, of the Kingdom of Heaven are not what I imagined.

I would have to surrender to You all my preconceived notions.

Dear Lord:

Please accept my filter. Please accept it as a burnt offering. Turn it to ash, and from these ashes the truth will rise.

Open my ears to listen, my eyes to see and my heart to receive.

Allow me to trust in You.

Allow me to accept the truth.

Allow me to sit in Your righteousness.

Allow me to experience Your love.

Amen

The Coat

The coat has been worn for years, and it shows its age. There are thin spots along the collar and cuffs, some frayed edges, and small tears along the seams. Faded and discoloured from the elements and permeated with the scent of the owner, not a foul odour just the smell of ownership. It has lost most of its insulating value and the zipper sticks now and again.

The new coat is everything the old coat is not.

Yet, I fear discarding the old. It is all I've ever known. I am leery of the new. Will it fit properly? Will it be comfortable? Will I be comfortable in it? Who will I be if I wear it? What will people say? Will they be jealous, envious, resentful, bitter? Will they recognize me?

Maybe I can wear the old coat over the new. I'll hide the new one, that way I can have both. A foolish and unrealistic thought, I know, but the old is all I've ever known.

Who will I be in the new? It is terrifying not knowing.

The time has come to remove and discard the old. The time has come to embrace the new. To wear it boldly, knowing the warmth and protection it provides, to inhale the scent of the Maker, to be thankful that I have been provided this opportunity.

It is time to make it mine.

The Anchor

In this vast body of water, I float along in my little rowboat. With no land in sight, rowing sometimes this way, sometimes that way, with no idea if they are the same direction or opposite directions, but at least I feel in control. I have oars, so I am the captain. I decide where I go, when I paddle and how fast or even if I wish to paddle at all.

I have no map, no instruments, no landmarks. I am navigating blindly.

I am at the mercy of the winds and the currents. I drift. Lost, directionless, not knowing where I am going or where I should be going.

The current gets stronger, the winds pick up and buffet my little boat. They come from various directions. I lose even the semblance of managing the situation. I am out of control as well as lost. HELP ME!

I throw the anchor in. Will it reach bottom? Will it catch and hold? Will the rope be strong enough? Will the knots hold?

All I can do is trust. Trust the anchor. Trust it will hold me.

Surrender

Hands clutched tight;
    Grasping, pulling, holding

Heart sealed off;
    Fortified, protected, safe

Mind made up;
    Logical, rational, worldly

To You, I surrender
To You, I open my hands
To You, I unseal my heart
To You, I release my mind
To You, I give all that I am

Obedience

I am just beginning to understand the meaning of this word.

What does it mean to obey? I've always viewed it as an authoritative command. A demand that is placed upon me with no options, no choices, no input. A set of actions on my part to fulfill the wishes of another. I've always hated the word. I may perform the prescribed action; but my heart remained resentful, hard, and despising of the order given. Not only hating the word, but hating the authority behind the word.

I would not be a puppet, a pawn. I would not participate. I would not bend to authority. I would rather break and maintain my autonomy.

Interestingly enough, I have never directly been asked to obey. I have been asked to listen. My response being "listen to what?" Many years later I am still learning to listen. To hear that still small voice. To listen with my ears, my eyes, all my senses and that is all good and well but the most important is to listen with my heart.

I have also been asked to trust. This has been a harder task to work through. I am distrustful and cynical by nature. My immediate response is defensive, self-protective. "What's your angle?" "What's in it for you?" "How am I being manipulated?" "If it's too good to be true, then it can't be true."

Trust is not something I give easily. It is earned over time through an understanding of what or whom I am trusting. I need to get to know You. This has been a long-term project. Through reading, praying, seeing, and experiencing how You work in my, and others', lives, an understanding of who You are is building. And with that, trust is growing as well.

I am beginning to see obey in a different light.

It is not the letter of the law You want, it is the spirit. A right heart and a right mind. (This is what Jesus was trying to explain to the Pharisees.) This is what I have needed to understand.

Obey comes from a surrendered heart that wants to follow. A heart filled with and overflowing with love and gratitude, with grace and joy. This is where obedience comes from.

This is what I am learning.

The Cliff

I stand at the edge of the cliff.

I am to jump – to trust completely.

I am afraid, so instead I climb down the face of the cliff. Bloody hands and feet. All exposed skin is scraped raw. Muscles tire. Exhaustion sets in. I cling to the rock face unable to move for months/years at a time.

Stuck.

Chronologically I age, but I do not grow. I struggle in my own effort and strength. I look up to see my progress – I have gone less than a body's length. I look down and cannot see the bottom. I am weary, discouraged, defeated in my own effort. No longer able to even inch downward. I desperately cling to the rock face.

Paralyzed.

It is not until I surrender and release my grip on the known. Letting go of what I am able to see and feel. Ready to trust completely. Then, I slowly turn and face the open air. Then I jump into the arms of Jesus as he had asked many years ago.

Liberated.

Redemption

I will sprinkle clean water on you, and you will be clean; I will cleanse you from all your impurities and from all your idols. I will give you a new heart and put a new spirit in you; I will remove from you your heart of stone and give you a heart of flesh. And I will put my spirit in you and move you to follow my decrees. I will save you from all your uncleanness.

Ezekiel 36; 25-29 (NIV)

The Gift

There in the centre of the room is the gift. A box with red ribbon around it and a bow on top. Just a nondescript gift box, not too big or too small. Just sitting there.

I know what is inside. I've been told. I've read about it. I know the gift has been given to me. I know each of us has been provided with this gift. Our choice is, do we open it, do we accept this gift? Each of us must answer this question ourselves.

I walk around the wrapped box, observing it from all angles. I poke at it... nothing happens. I walk around it the other way... no change. I sit cross legged in front of it, elbows on knees, my head resting in my hands, watching the gift, contemplating... nothing changes. Time ticks... and still I watch.

If I open the box, everything changes and it can't go back to the way it was.

If I don't open the box, nothing changes, everything remains the same.

Within the box, there are promises. Beautiful, meaningful and love-filled promises.

I've observed the gift from all sides, I've heard of others who have opened their gift and the wonderfully awesome things that lie within. Why have I not opened mine?

It is not a holiday or special occasion. It is not something I worked for or am being rewarded for. I definitely don't deserve it. If I open it, will I be expected to act or behave in a certain way? Will I be expected to pay back in equal value? Will I be beholden to the gift giver? I have nothing in kind to be able to pay back. I have always fallen short of expectations – would this be any different?

The Gift Giver says it is free to all – no exceptions. This gift is not forced upon me. It is my choice to accept or reject as I wish.

I know of no example in this world that works this way. It is not of this world. **"I (God) don't think the way you think. The way you work isn't the way I (God) work." Isaiah 55:8 (MSG)**

Which brings us back to trust.

"If you then, though you are evil, know how to give good gifts to your children, how much more will your Father in heaven give the Holy Spirit to those who ask him!" Luke 11:13 (NIV)

Each of us has the gift available to us:

Some are not aware that the gift is for them personally

Some are not aware a gift is available

Some reject the gift

Some distrust the gift

Some think the gift is not real

Some hide the gift

Some carry the gift but never open it

Some place the gift in a special place, but never take it out of the box.

I will open my gift. My fingers tremble with excitement, anticipation and mixed with a hint of nervousness. Inside is the most beautiful, luxurious item I have ever seen. A dark, royal blue that shimmers in the light. The softest, strongest most plush feeling material – nothing compares that I have touched before. I lift it out of the gift wrap.

It is a floor length robe lined with the finest silk-like material, It is trimmed in a soft white fur-like material. It is so lightweight it feels like it floats in my hands. I wrap it around my shoulders. Of course it fits perfectly, it was made specifically for me! A sense of regalness overwhelms me. I stand taller. All sense of heaviness within me is gone.

Half-Buried

It lies half-buried

A misshapen blackened lump

Cold, dead, discarded

Unvalued and worthless

At first only a few stray strands of light reach it

As the day progresses the beams become stronger

Gently caressing and smoothing the roughened form

Melting the filth and dirt that encases and restricts the beauty
that lies within

The brilliantly pure light penetrates to its epicentre

Stirring a warmth not known before

And with this any remnants of its worldly covering is shaken off

It radiates the light it has been provided

A deep unblemished red

A strong life-giving pulse flows through it

The heart is free

Stone Fountain

A tiered stone fountain sits in the middle of the meadowland – a natural beauty surrounds it. Blue sky with wisps of white clouds float in the clear and bright air overhead. The sounds of nature emanate from the forest that encompasses the meadowlands. Wild flowers bloom in all their brilliance. The scene is perfection, with no signs of manicuring or order.

The crystallized sounds of running water are overheard above those of the natural world surrounding the fountain. They beckon all that come near. Come, **"Taste and see that the Lord is good;" Psalm 34:8 (NIV)**

There is a disturbance at the edge of the forest as a person comes running forward. Full tilt. Are they running from or are they running to? They full-body throw themselves into the water. Drinking deeply, splashing, laughing, dancing around the stone tiers. Filling themselves deeply, resting fully, pure and utter bliss covers their face. Wild abandon and care free.

Opposite to where this took place there are others standing at the edge of the forest cautiously stepping toward the fountain as well. Wary, glancing sideways and over their shoulder. Slowly they approach. Each timid step – calls us to encourage them. When they reach the edge of the fountain, they stand looking at the falling water, the glistening surface of bubbles and ripples. They pull a thimble from their pocket and dip into the water being careful not to get their fingers wet. And take a small sip of the life giving substance. The sweetness of it putting a smile to their lips. They turn and walk away.

My Walk

I've been walking for some time. During the time I've been walking I have gathered many articles. Some I've picked up myself, some have been given to me, some thrust upon me. But always I accept. I just add them on like pieces of clothing. I am now wearing layers and layers; short and long underwear, tights, numerous pairs of pants and overalls, so many pairs of socks I've lost count, shoes, oversized boots and galoshes, undershirts, tee shirts, long sleeve shirts, button-on shirts, sweaters, jackets and coats, neck warmers and a multitude of scarves, gloves, mitts, and hats, piled one on top the other.

It has become difficult to walk. It is a labour to put one foot in front of the other. The heat is stifling, the air stale. It is difficult to see and hear through these layers, and still I walk on. At least I am safe and protected…but isolated and lonely.

As I walk I am joined by a fellow traveller. He asks if he can walk along side me. I don't think he hears my muffled "I don't care." He slows his pace to mine and we walk in silence. At times I don't think he is there, that he has moved on, that I am alone.

Great distances are travelled like this. Most of the time I forget that he is there, matching his step with mine. It startles me when I look over and see him still there.

Eventually I ask, "Why are you still here?" He just smiles and continues to walk with me. Gradually, I'm not sure when it happened, but it became comfortable to have a fellow traveller with me. Every so often I'd make a comment. Mostly he'd just smile and continue by my side.

Once, I said this journey is difficult and I am finding it hard to carry on. He offered to carry some pieces of clothing for me. I thought long and hard about this – as these were my burdens, it wasn't someone else's responsibility. I politely declined the offer and continued to trudge along.

On one particularly difficult day, I fell to my hands and knees and could not get back up. I was ready to just stay there. To lie down, roll over, and give up. Again he offered to carry my burdensome layers. This time I said, "Yes, thank you."

Layer after layer of clothing was removed – as he removed my layers he put them on himself. Eventually I was able to stand back up with his help. I was free of the heavy restrictive layers. I could move, I could breathe fresh air, I could see and hear. It was the most wonderful sensation.

I looked over at my fellow traveller. I could not see the layers of my clothes he had put on. Most curious. He again smiled that loving, caring smile that radiated into his face and most importantly into his eyes. If you tilted your head just right you could see a soft glow surrounding him.

We are continuing to travel together – his pace matching mine. The steps are much lighter now. We converse, laugh, and cry together. There are still periods where we walk in silence, but it is a comfortable silence.

And I wouldn't have it any other way.

Circle

Each of us created with the Lord's powerful self-expression

Each of us created as an individual

Each of us unique

Each of us a special treasure

> The Architect of the Universe lovingly and passionately formed us. Placing a holy piece of Spirit within each of us.

When we are ready, when we ask, You allow Your heart and soul to reveal itself. You allow the beauty and brilliance from within to shine, enlightening both us and those around us. Exposing us all, to who You are.

> This journey of self-exploration brings us full circle back to our creator – being redeemed back to You.

Christ in Me

If Christ is in me, then I am able to claim the qualities of Christ, for they also reside in me.

If the Holy Spirit has been given as a gift when Christ left earth, then I am able to access that gift.

I have the courage and confidence of Christ in me.

I have the strength and wisdom of Christ in me.

I have the love and patience of Christ in me.

I have the living light of Christ in me.

I claim these qualities and graciously accept them as the gift You bestow on the world. I just need to let go of me (to surrender) and let You shine through.

Faithfulness

Because of the Lord's great love we are not
consumed, for his compassions never fail.
They are new every morning;
Great is your faithfulness.

Lamentations 3 : 22&23 (NIV)

Leave and Forsake

My greatest fear is that You will
    Leave me and forsake me.

Yet You promise
    "I will never leave you nor forsake you."

Please do not
    Leave me nor forsake me.

Please do not turn Your face from me!

    I need You more than air itself.

Where are You?

I turn to You in times of trouble. Sometimes I feel Your presence and sometimes I feel utterly alone, abandoned. Yet You tell me "I will never leave you or forsake you," so why can't I feel You?

I wish to experience Your presence, to wear it like a favourite sweater or blanket. To wrap myself in it, and be surrounded by Your warmth, to feel protected, safe and secure. To not only know You are there but to feel that You are there. I want the sensation of Your presence. I want it to be a part of me. I want it wherever I walk.

Ah, but there is the rub. I want it where I walk. Always I struggle for a sense of independence. Rebellion resides within me. I resist. When You are close I become comfortable, complacent, think myself special, and lean towards arrogance and pride.

When Your presence is far from me, I look for You, leaving my ways to seek Yours. I am desperate to find You. I turn to Your direction. I wish to find the route You are on, only wanting to be with You.

How many times will I stray?

How many times will I fall away?

How many times will you open Your arms and receive me back into Your fold?

When will I learn?

My Prayer

(Paraphrased from NIV)
Psalm 51 verses 8, 10 -12

Let me hear joy and gladness

Create in me a pure heart

Renew a steadfast spirit within me

Do not cast me from Your presence

Or take Your Holy Spirit from me

Restore to me the joy of Your salvation

And grant me a willing spirit to sustain me

Amen

Mirror

Like a mirror, I can only reflect the light You provide.

When my face remains turned towards You – Your light is brilliant, radiating all it touches.

When my face turns from You, I have no light to reflect and the world becomes dull and dark.

Your light is always ready, always shining.

Waiting for us to turn to You.

Waiting for us to be bathed in Your radiant glow.

Waiting for us to reflect what we are given.

Waiting for us to follow Your light wherever it shines.

Waiting for us to keep our face turned toward You.

I Know You are There

When speaking to You quietly

Laying my heart bare...

I know You are there.

When driving in noisy congested traffic

Or winding through lonely country lanes...

I know You are there.

When breaking bread

With family and friends...

I know You are there.

When performing menial tasks

Like housework, yardwork and errands...

I know You are there.

When comforting others

With cut fingers, hurt feelings or broken hearts...

I know You are there.

When acting mean-spirited
With hurtful actions and words...
I know You are there.

When filled with the emotions
Of anger, guilt and remorse...
I know You are there.

When experiencing
heartache, grief and despair...
I know You are there.

When I turn from You, When I turn to You
When I strike at You, When I run to You
When I cry, When I laugh
When I am loud, When I am quiet
When I am self-righteous, When I am God-righteous
No matter what, when, where or how...
You are always there.

The Mustard Seed

The mustard seed of faith has lain dormant for years. It was planted long ago. Waiting

Surrounded by the noise of the world. The cares, the worries, the busyness of everyday struggles. They are the weeds that choke it.

So it lay dormant... Waiting

The demands of schedules, of work, of family and friends pushed the seed to the background where not water nor light nor fertile ground reached it.

So it lay dormant... Waiting

Everywhere around us we are told how to fit in, how to be accepted. The protocol and procedures of living your life to be part of this society framed by human hands and expectations. They tried to carry my seed of faith away.

But it lay dormant... Waiting

It waited until I chose to give my everyday struggles to You.

It waited until I chose to make time for You each and every day.

It waited until I chose to see Your kingdom, Your instructions, and Your guidance for a full life.

It waited until I chose to accept Your love, fully, completely and without condition.

That was the time the mustard seed of faith grew... and grew... **and grew!**

From the centre of my being it spreads out surrounding each cell in my body. Bringing light and love and hope with it.

Reaching my heart, my head, my hands, and my feet. Permeating and bringing my complete self to life.

It is at peace, fully content and fully alive. Filled with harmony, with hope and with joy.

It feels a sense of oneness that comes with complete surrender.

It is what I have searched for all my life and it has been with me the whole time... Waiting.

Forgiveness

Bear with each other and forgive whatever grievances you may have against one another. Forgive as the Lord forgave you.

Colossians 3:13 (NIV)

Dagger to the Heart

Like a dagger to the heart it is.

Whether it is the rejection of a loved one, the abuse of a parent or spouse, the betrayal of a friend, the loss of a child to rebellion or death, or the random life changing act of a stranger. It becomes buried deep within us. There it festers and grows and consumes who we once were, and morphs us into someone unrecognizable, carrying anger, bitterness, hurt, and tears. We cling to the emotions as they provide a reason for putting one foot in front of the other. We turn into a resentful, empty shell of a person. We hang on to the pain as it gives purpose. It provides sympathy and human understanding.

But the consuming hatred of unfairness eats us from the inside out. Our sole purpose becomes one of revenge, of the justice of an eye for an eye.

Even if someone does pay, gets what's coming to them, and they end up hurt either physically, emotionally, financially, or psychologically, it is never enough. It still does not match our pain and hurt. It does not heal the wound to our heart.

The dagger needs to be removed, and it needs to be given away. And only you can give it away. It will not be taken from you otherwise. You must let go before true healing can begin.

Many will not understand, many will question, they may even turn against your choice to let go, encouraging you to hang on to the pain causing burden and seek vengeance.

But Trust

Let go

Release

Forgive

Be healed

Be free

What Might Have Been

I stand on the edge of the rugged coast line watching the ship sail away. As it recedes into the horizon the missed opportunity grows in my mind. The image blurs, I blink and the fat tears drop silently to the ground. I grieve.

I replay the scenario, grasping at the reasons... if only he had... if only she had... if only they had... if only, if only, if only..., then it would all be different. Perfect.

With each replay I see better the part they played, their responsibility for ruining it for me. I see the blame they should, no, HAVE to accept. They did it wrong, I was right. I am blameless. With each replay I breathe life into the shadow of what could have been. The shadow eventually becomes a dark dense fog. With each acrid thought the rationale for my anger, bitterness, and resentment grows. The acid bile of emotion feeds on its self, corroding all it touches, eating me from the inside out.

That other person is responsible!

That other person is to blame!

That other person should hurt like I do!

That other person should have to pay!

It's not fair!!

My hateful emotions give me strength; allowing me to continue to stand tall at the edge of the rugged coast line, allowing me to continue to replay the image of the ship sailing away, allowing me to vocalize how I was wronged, allowing my feet to remain stationary in this spot, allowing me to be perpetually trapped. Trapped in the past of what could have been, would should have been. What I imagined to be my perfect life.

Yes Lord, I know vengeance and justice are Yours.

Yes Lord, I know You hold me in the palm of Your hand.

Yes Lord, I know You have plans to prosper me and not to harm me.

Yes Lord, I know You love all Your children.

Yes Lord, I know I must repent.

Yes Lord, I know I must forgive.

Yes Lord, I know I must let go, to surrender it all to You.

Dear Lord: I give You my grief, my anger, my resentment, and bitterness. I don't need them to hold me upright. I have You to lean on. You are my strength.

Dear Lord: I give You my plans, the direction, and route. I hand over the belief that I am in the driver's seat. I will follow where You lead.

Dear Lord: I hand over my shadow-clouded thoughts of blame. I release those I have held responsible for my anger and pain to You. I no longer wish to sit in judgment. The throne is Yours. Please forgive me, as I forgive them.

Dear Lord: Please release my feet. Allow me to turn. To turn my back on what might have been, to turn and face my future of what will be. To turn to You.

Ball of String

You have given me a ball of string. You hold one end and as I travel the string unwinds. I go as I please – here and there – back and forth – around and about. It is not long before there is a tangled mess of knots and loops. It looks like many strings not just one continuous strand. I try to go back to untangle the mess I made, to make it right again. I work at it, concentrating, unravelling a bit here but that makes it worse over there. My focus is completely on where I have been, on the knots, on the loops and on the tangles.

When I hit my wall of frustration, the point where I realize I cannot do it, the point of surrender, I call on You. I lay my heart bare, (so I think), explaining how this mess happened, rationalizing why it's not my fault, trying to shine the best light on my behaviour, and although You are listening, I know You are not buying it.

I stop.

I look up and with tears rolling down my face and holding nothing back I simply say – 'I'm Sorry.'

I sense the delight in You. And with those three little words the knots, the loops, the tangled mess that is within me is released. I am freed from the web of my own making.

It is when I walk close with You – listening to Your directions, watching the paths You point out – that is when my ball of string unravels easily, knot-free and tangle-free.

What is Seen

The physical eye sees only the red beating heart

A strong muscular contraction that creates a regular rhythm

The pulsation of blood flow through the vessels

All appears healthy and well

The spiritual eye sees it differently

A darkness coats the heart, choking it

But not just coating also intertwining – like a fungus seeping into the muscle itself

Living off it and strangling it at the same time

Please Lord,

Remove this cloak of darkness that surrounds my heart. Forgive my invitation to it and release me. I wish to be healthy and whole and a true child of Yours.

Transformation

When Moses came down from Mount Sinai... He was not aware that his face was radiant because he had spoken with the Lord.

Exodus 34 : 29 (NIV)

Burrs

Each time I come to You   Burdened and weary
                                        Discouraged and hurting.

You receive my pitiful offerings of pain and tears, my fears and failures.

I leave refreshed, full of hope and expectation.

But as I walk through this world, the dust of it blurs my vision and chokes my breath and I fall lockstep into the pattern of those around me. I pick up the problems and the concerns and the worries, making those challenges mine as well. Carrying them with me, allowing them to stoop my shoulder, slow my step and draw my eye to the ground. My focus limited to the next step.

Again, I return to You, giving You the worldly problems that I have gathered. They stick to me like burrs: irritating, like an itch that can't be scratched. They are small but are consuming, demanding my attention. Their smallness competes with Your greatness.

Why do I let them win?

Why do I keep walking through burrs?

Why do I let them cling to me?

Lord, how do I walk with You so I am not covered in worldly dust at the end of the day? How do I live in this world with You in my heart? How do I experience Your fruits when I'm covered in burrs?

I am tired of this repeating pattern, Please show me how to do it differently!

"...stand firm, then, and do not let yourselves be burdened again by a yoke of slavery." Galatians 5:1 (NIV)

Growing Pains

Excitement, Trial, Failure
Never mind, Try again

Enthusiasm, Trial, Failure
You can do it, Try again

Nervous anticipation, Trial, Failure
It's okay, Try again

Trepidation, Trial, Failure
Brush it off, Try again

Apprehension, Trial, Failure
I can't do it!!

"I know, dear child, but together
WE can... follow Me"

(We cannot follow when we are running ahead)

Two Ways

The pathway was wide enough for two people to walk side by side. It was ramp-like in nature, gently rising from the surrounding terrain. Eagerly I walked on it, progressing both forward and upward. Gradually a crack appeared in the centre of the path. Widening as I travelled. At first it was simple to straddle. Then as it widened, to step across to where the path was easiest to travel. All the while, the way forward and upward narrowed on each side and continued to rise higher from the ground below. Soon I was jumping from side to side. Unable to choose, unable to decide, unable to commit. Forward progress stalled and become static as the movement was now horizontal. I tried to inch forward with the sideways movement, but it was laborious and defeating. Yet, I continued trying to have it both ways. Eventually I fell into the crack and tumbled to the bottom of my indecision, trapped, lost, and in the dark.

At times I would try to scramble out – only to fall back. Lying depleted of both energy and will. A lost soul filled only with self-pity. Months turned to years and they in turn became decades.

At times, fragments would fall down around me. At first I was beyond caring, just waiting to rot, to become one with the earthen floor. The fragments continued to rain down.

You are loved

You have been saved

You are my child

Grabbing hold of these words, looking upward for their source a ray of hope seeped its way inside me. I stood and actively began searching skyward for more.

You are mine

You cannot be separated from my love

I will guide you

Follow me

Let me heal you

Give your burdens to me

I am the way, the truth and the light

So I followed, eventually finding myself back on the divided pathway. The place I had been at when I fell into the gap.

A choice was in front of me. Pick a path. Trying to walk both did not work. On one path I could now see the world that I knew. On the other the one that saved me.

You would think it a no-brainer, easy as pie. But if that was the case everyone would be on the same path. What I know vs the unknown. Relying on myself vs trusting You. Independence vs obedience. I have not found it easy; I have found it a struggle, but wanting both and having neither has been a living hell.

I choose life!

Yes! I will follow the One that loves me!

Yes! I will walk into the unknown, trusting and obeying the One that rescued me!

My heart is filled with gratitude!

My heart is filled with the love that You have given me!

My heart sings to You and commits to You!

Caterpillar, Chrysalis, Butterfly

The Caterpillar

    Unquenchable hunger

    Unquenchable consumption

    Unquenchable self-focus

    Unquenchable destruction

    Unquenchable purpose

**"... whoever drinks the water I give him will never thirst."
John 4:14 (NIV)**

The Chrysalis

    A time of consolidation

    A time of stillness

    A time of external stasis

    A time of internal transition

    A time of transformation

"Be still, and know that I am God;" Psalm 46:10 (NIV)

The Butterfly

> Pinnacle of maturity

> Pinnacle of potential

> Pinnacle of purpose

> Pinnacle of beauty

> Pinnacle of love

"... if we love one another, God lives in us and his love is made complete in us." 1 John 4:12 (NIV)

Fill Me

I beg You, I plead to You, I implore You

Fill Me!

Fill me as I am

Incomplete without You

Fill the spaces around my cells

Fill the empty cavities

Fill the space within each atom

Fill them with:

Your love

Your peace

Your kindness

Your gentleness

Your joy

Your self-discipline

Your patience

Your goodness

Your faithfulness

As I have none of my own

Come Holy Spirit

Then I will be complete

Then I will be whole

Die to Self

How does one die to self?

It is exhausting trying to keep my worlds apart. An internal struggle, no not struggle… battle, I've been waging for years. Like a pendulum – back and forth, back and forth. Constant momentum but no progress, no growth. Static – caught in a continuous pattern. Back and forth, back and forth, back and forth.

Swing towards You, gain speed, then slow as I get closer, get too close and fear sets in, stop and head back to my worldly desires – run towards the way of life I've always known. The further I go from You, the more I want You, desire You, need You. Again I slow, then stop, and go racing back towards You.

Again, and again, and again, and again, and again, I repeat this ongoing pattern. It wears, it exhausts, it depletes. Until I am nothing but a shell. Repeating the only pattern I know. It disgusts me and yet I continue.

I want, wish, desire You to remove the lynch pin of this pendulum. Yet I fear: Will I fall? Will You catch me? Will I lose everything I love? Will I lose everything I know? Will I be lost?

Logically I know the answers to these questions – well some of them, I think.

I am afraid.

My fear holds me back. It binds me to a living purgatory. I lack courage. I lack strength. I lack faith. Mostly I lack trust.

I beseech You. (Beseech, what a wonderful word; plead, beg, wanton desire, and helplessness rolled into one)

I beseech You, help me overcome. Rescue me from myself. Save me from this perpetual hell.

Purpose

Without You I am an empty shell. Hungering and searching for fulfillment, for purpose, for peace and contentment.

I've tried filling the void with relationships, both romantic and platonic, but neither satisfies I just hunger for more – so I continue to search.

I've tried pouring myself into career and volunteering; but neither fulfills the starving void. Only a feeling of exhaustion and drained emptiness in place of the fullness I desire – so I continue to search.

I've tried material wealth: things, property and expensive vacations. Each lasting but a moment in time, soon to become boring and complacent, and then searching for the next best thing. Wanting more and more in the hope that the next item will be what provides the fulfillment that I'm searching for. But they are empty dreams – so I continue to search.

It was not until You heard the heart song of my soul. Only You knew what I was looking for, what I was longing for, what I was missing and desiring. Only You could satisfy my hunger, provide the peace and contentment that I have so restlessly desired. Only You define my purpose of being: to be loved by You, and through that bountiful and overflowing love being able to love others.

To truly love without the expectation of anything in return.

To be able to accept Your gift and in turn give that gift to others.

This is my purpose, this is my reason for being created: To Be Loved and To Love.

Broken Vessels

I have heard that we are described as broken vessels.

Are we born broken? And become aware of it as life proceeds? Or are we born whole then chip and crack with time, experiences and choices? Or is it some of both?

I presently see my chips, breaks, cracks and holes – but do I see all of them? Or is there more to be revealed? Lately, I've become aware of this brokenness and wonder if there are enough sound parts left to make a complete vessel again.

The tears I've cried within this vessel mingle with the tears of Jesus as he grieves with me. It happens so slowly that the changes are not perceived. Over time, this mixture of tears crystallizes in the cracks, chips, breaks and holes. They are filled with both small and large crystals.

My tears alone create a one-dimensional salt crystal. Jesus' tears have provided multi-dimensional healing to this vessel that is me. It is this mixture that has created the completely unique and whole vessel that I am.

This vessel can show its uniqueness and beauty only when the light resides within. The light that shines from the vessel's interior can then flood out creating a kaleidoscope of colour through the healed brokenness of crystallized tears.

Your Love Rains Down

Your love rains down upon me

Large fat drops

I open my mouth wide

Head tilted skyward

The sweetest taste

It quenches

It satisfies

It fills

Greedily, I lap up each drop not wanting to let even
one hit the ground

Each drop that touches my skin moistens my dry exterior

I am surrounded, refreshed and cleansed by Your love

I am content

Sitting in peace

Enjoying Your reign

The Flame

An immense, roaring, incomprehensible, burning fire rages all around us.

Can you see it? Can you hear it? Can you feel it? Can you sense it at all?

What about the spark, the ember, the flame?

Do you recognize the tinier bits?

This is what can reside in us, just a small piece of a greater whole.

To be transformed by this all-consuming flame.

To burn away the impurities.

Turning sin and guilt to ash to be blown away in the wind.

To be refined, smelted into something more than we once were.

To be shaped into Your image, but to be so much more than an image.

To be a living, breathing part of You.

To have that eternal flame burning internally.

An I for an Aye

I, eye, aye

What is seen by I

What is interpreted by I

I, I, I

See the transformation

See the Sea that rocks you

See the Rock that floats upon the Sea

Stand upon the Rock

Eye, Eye, Eye

Ewe the Mother of the Lamb

You the Father of the Lamb

The Lamb that is the Rock

The foundation of my Soul

Aye, Aye, Aye

Who God Is

God said to Moses,
"I AM WHO I AM."

Exodus 3: 14 (NIV)

Created in Your Image

To be created in Your image. What does that mean?

A reflection?

A photocopy?

A mirage?

A figment?

Is the image

Physical?

Mental?

Emotional?

We take that little line "Let us make human beings in our image," Genesis 1:26 (MSG) and try to reverse engineer You. We try to make You in our image.

And we end up making You small, and petty, and insignificant. And we say there; That is who God is! Just like us! Aren't we wonderful?

But, what if the image we were created in was God's heart?

That we are given the capacity to love as God loves us?

That we are able to forgive and embrace each other as God forgives and embraces us?

That we are able to be filled with compassion and empathy for each other as God has compassion and empathy for us?

That we are able to have patience and provide encouragement for each other as God is patient and encourages us?

That we are able to accept each other, meeting others where they are at and encouraging them to grow into their better selves as God meets us where we are at and encourages us to grow into our best selves?

That is the created image I long to be.

Fire

Fire: how indispensable to our lives. Providing heat, protection, the ability to cook, to sterilize, refine metals, create glass, cauterize wounds, but only when it is contained, small, controlled.

It must be treated with respect, with caution and a knowledge of its potential.

The ability to be a raging inferno, to burn, to hurt, to destroy, to be large, uncontrollable, creating its own weather and feeding system.

I think we try to treat God like fire. By keeping it small, contained and under our control, not fully understanding or knowing its' full potential. Not realizing this fire is its own master. Not fearing the Lord.

Who am I

You cannot fail the Lord

God knows who you are

We only fail the expectations of ourselves

The expectations we place upon ourselves

God knows who we are better than we could ever know ourselves

We build false projections of who we think we should be for the world to see

To that end we are constantly living a lie

It leads to disappointment, shame, guilt and unhappiness

Please Lord,

Help me see myself as You see me. Show me who I am. Lead me to the person who You know me to be. Destroy my false projections. Lead me to life, love, and truth. Reveal the beauty that lies within.

Words

Words are like water.

Words mould the landscape of our being.

Words can cut pathways through a dry and parched land. They can create channels and gullies. Following the path of what came before. Words can carve a deep and entrenched system of understanding within us.

Words can be life-sustaining.

Gently bathing us, uplifting us, peacefully floating us, and suspending our troubles. Words can wash away our hurts and grief. Release us from the pull of gravity – from worldly worries and earthly anchors.

Words can be life-destroying.

Words can be harsh and driving, causing a burning sensation from their force. Words can cut us, and leave us wounded. Words can flood us with emotion, drowning and demolishing whatever lies in their path. Words can pound us with wave upon wave, eroding us, and in the process forming something different, something new and unrecognizable.

Your Word quenches our thirst. Your Word replenishes our soul. Sustains us, re-hydrates us. Your Word tastes so sweet, cleansing us from within.

Your Word waters the garden of our souls, providing green growth, the blooming of fruit – character and moral fibre, the blossoming of our righteous selves. The fragrance of which fills the air around us. The delectable smells drawing in those who are near us. Your Word is an invitation to those to see the beautiful garden of who we are. All thanks to the living water of Your Word.

Eternal Life

Not the empty hollow shell of monotonous, ongoing, never-ending trudging experience of what I have been living:

But a bubbling, wellspring of overflowing abundance.

Not endless, sameness of time in a straight line:

But of each moment packed with the fullness of a loving God. Pure saturation of joy, peace, and contentment.

Eternal is not a timeline or a forward progression of movement:

But a timeless moment of being totally fulfilled.

It is not gained or won:

But exists within us.

All that is needed is to sit quietly and experience Christ within us, to accept what already is.

You Are The One

You are the One who gives me strength

You are the One who heals me

You are the One who gives me courage

You are the One who eases my pain

You are the One who forgives me

You are the One who quiets my fears

You are the One who extinguishes my anxious thoughts

You are the One who calms me

You are the One who holds me in the palm of your hand

You are the One who stills my trembling

You are the One who is in control

You are the One who is all powerful

You are the One I hand myself over to

You are the One I will open myself to

You are the One I trust

You are the One I love

Love Says

Pride Says:	Brokenness Says:	Love Says:
I can climb the mountain	I can't get out of the valley	You are never alone
I am in control of my life	I have lost control of my life	You do not know the plans I have for you
I am the master of my fate	I am a slave to my circumstances	You are my child
I earn my way	I am always failing	To you I have given a child, His name is Emmanuel

Thankfulness

But you are a chosen people, a royal priesthood, a holy nation, a people belonging to God, that you may declare the praises of him who called you out of darkness into his wonderful light.

1 Peter 2: 9 (NIV)

Morning Song

It is early

Dawn just breaking

The landscape featureless

The silhouette of trees stark against the gradients of blue sky

A narrow band of pale pink on the horizon

The brightest of stars remain

The day is filled with expectation

Like a new birth

The anticipation of what this day holds grows as the
sky lightens

The odd combination of excitement and peace resides
in harmony

The faint building of today's song is beginning

Each of us with a note to play in today's symphony

Each of us partaking in the creation of this beautiful day

I will sing my note bright and clear and strong

How will you sing yours?

Because

Because I am loved, I am able to love

Because I am forgiven, I am able to forgive

Because I am given gifts, I am able to give

Because I am accepted, I am able to accept

Because I AM showed me kindness, I am able to be kind

Because I AM showed me respect, I am able to give respect

Because I AM showed me understanding, I am able to
give understanding

Because I AM showed love to a sinner, I am able to
love myself

Because I AM was, is and will be; I am able to be whom I was
created to be

                    … I AM's Child

Thank you

Thank you Lord Jesus;

> For rescuing me from my pit of
> self-despair

Thank you Lord Jesus;

> For your beautiful radiant light that
> you shine upon me and from within me

Thank you Lord Jesus;

> For your grace-filled forgiveness

I love you so much and with my whole heart

"My Beautiful Child"

This is what my God calls me

My – I belong, I am accepted, I am God's possession

Beautiful – How God sees me. Looking beyond the behaviour and action to what lies within. Who I truly am

Child – A family member. Something larger than myself, still needing growth, maturity, guidance, and direction

How powerful is this, to understand who I am:

Your Beautiful Child!

Wealth

Wealth – I have it beyond my wildest dreams

>   You cannot see it or count it

>   There is no bank statement

>   There are no records of transactions

>   No bonds nor stocks

>   No cash, coins nor gems

>   No property nor possessions

>   Nothing of monetary value

My wealth is more precious than that. It cannot be bought or sold. It was given to me as a free gift – an inheritance.

>   It is a peace that passes all understanding

>   It is a freedom from all burdens, worries or concerns

>   It is a knowledge that you are never alone

>   It is a feeling of protection and care

>   It is a love so deep, so strong and so enduring that words are inadequate

>   It makes you weep just thinking about it

Jesus provides this wealth

I have neither worked for nor earned it; I have received it

Will you receive yours?

The Shore

Where sea meets land

Where water meets sand

The transition of me and real

The transition to You and ethereal

A magical place where two worlds reside

A magnetic place where the call's to abide

"Yes" to the sea I talk

But yes on the land I walk

Where the two are one

Where freely I run

A Final Message

I pray that out of his glorious riches he may strengthen you with power through his Spirit in your inner being, so that Christ may dwell in your hearts. And I pray that you, being rooted and established in love, may have power, to grasp how wide and long and high and deep is the love of Christ, and to know this love that surpasses knowledge – that you may be filled to the measure of all the fullness of God.

Ephesians 3: 16-19 (NIV)

Sea of Trouble

The sea is filled with bodies, drowning souls as far as the eye can see. Some have hands outstretched reaching upwards. Some no longer care to reach out. Some have eyes so dull they are blind to their plight. Some are looking toward the small boat in this large sea focusing on the single figure standing in it. He has an undefined light shimmering around, on, and from him.

He reaches out and pulls the outstretched hands into the boat, one at a time. Each person that enters the boat is wrapped in a blanket of warmth, of protection, of love, of forgiveness, and of acceptance.

He gently wipes the dirt and muck from their eyes that they may see him. He gently removes the seaweed and pushes back the water-soaked hair from their ears that they may hear the song he is singing to them.

He bends down kissing their foreheads, blessing them, and healing the shattered hearts, the torn and tattered emotions, the beaten and broken minds.

There is one that stands out. She is hearing his song. She is seeing him clearly. She remains wrapped in his blanket. She receives both his blessing and his healing.

She is the one who will remain in the boat with him. Helping to rescue those who are drowning in this sea of trouble.

"Hosea put it well: I'll call nobodies and make them somebodies;
I'll call the unloved and make them beloved.
In the place where they yelled out 'You're nobody!' they're calling you 'God's living children.'" Romans 9:25-26 (MSG)

My question to you: Will you allow yourself to be rescued?

Eventually I did, and this was my journey.

Do you even know you need to be rescued?

I thought I was beyond rescue, and yet, I was saved.